HOW TO CREATE A MONEY MAGNET MINDSET

HOW TO CREATE A MONEY MAGNET MINDSET

ANDREW LAYCOCK

© Andrew Laycock 2022. All rights reserved.

Any redistribution or reproduction of part or all of the contents in any form is prohibited without the express written permission of the copyright owner.

You may not, except with the express written permission of the copyright owner, distribute or commercially exploit the content. Nor may you transmit it or store it in any other website or other form of electronic retrieval system.

Contents

Introduction 1

Mindset 3

Belief 10

Vision 18

Behaviours 23

Actions 27

Momentum 36

Value 39

Alignment 41

Evaluation 49

INTRODUCTION

Empty pockets never held anyone back. Only empty heads and empty hearts can do that. –Norman Vincent Peale

We can all attract money. Every single one of us can become a money magnet if that is what we choose to be. Prosperity and abundance are not reserved for the rich and famous. There is no magic formula or secret ingredient known solely by the uber-wealthy. There is just a simple, universal law that states what we focus on, we receive.

When we set our minds on something, we do it. The world is full of people who achieved extraordinary things because they decided to. It's not easy, nor necessarily straightforward, but if we set our mind to do something and take action to achieve it, then we can. Those who fail only do so because they didn't want it badly enough, did not have a dream that consumed every waking thought or gave up at the sight of an obstacle.

Attracting money, becoming rich, and achieving the wealth and prosperity we want and deserve, is no different to focusing on and achieving whatever else we want in life. In the pages of this book, I will show you the steps you need to take to become a money magnet. You being the operative word. It's down to you, and you have to put the effort in. There is more to being a money magnet than waking up one day, deciding you want to be rich, and putting it out there to the Universe, although some books suggest that can be done. Yes, the Universe can help, but it helps those who help themselves. Those who not only believe in the power of thought, but translate those thoughts into action to create the reality that they want

I can't tell you how it works. It just does. In this day and age, when the world is open to us like never before, where every square inch of our planet is photographed and shown, we think we know it all. Our lives are laid bare on social media, and every decision we make and every thought we have is not only analysed by us but judged by others. We have been told that what can't be explained or seen cannot exist. We can't see the energy around us, so the belief that we can harness this energy to attract abundance to our lives is derided as the views of cranks or con artists.

I've been called both in my time, and many other names, but the reality is I'm neither. I'm happy to share my views in my training courses and books, but you don't have to read them or listen to them. Scientific facts back up nothing of what I write, but my beliefs do not come just from my brain but from my intuition and soul. And the scientific community has a hard time finding evidence for those, too, even though the consensus amongst most people is that they exist.

Are you willing to be an explorer and experiment, let go of the old ways of thinking and open your mind to new ideas? The information in this book can help you live your dream life, a life filled with wealth and abundance, where you attract money to you like a magnet attracts metal. This book will give you the tools and the methods to make positive changes to your life. Remember, though, that you are changing and transforming a lifetime of old beliefs and habits, which you cannot achieve overnight. But stick with it, and you truly can achieve the lifestyle and the prosperity you deserve.

Mindset

The mind is everything. What you think you become. —Buddha

Our mindset is the established set of attitudes that govern how we think. It differs significantly from our personality, which are the characteristics that control how we behave, although many people confuse the two. It is tough to change our personality in the short term, although the situations we find ourselves in and the events that happen to us may cause our personality to change over time. It is easy to change our mindset very quickly, though, because we can control our thoughts completely.

Imagine for a moment that you wanted to lose weight. You love food. Your whole social life revolves around food. Eating good food and drinking fine wine is one of your favourite pastimes. A night out with friends tends to start in a restaurant. A get-together with the girls happens over a pizza and several gin and tonics. Birthdays always involve a cake. A picnic basket goes with you on a long car journey, and meals with the extended family invariably run to several courses. Is that love of food going to change because you want to lose weight?

Of course, it isn't. Your love of food will not disappear because you want to lose weight. Your love of food is part of who you are, yet even the most ardent lover of food does not have to resign themselves to being overweight for the rest of their life. You can love food and still lose weight because you can control your mindset. You can exercise the emotional powers that control your mindset, like you can exercise your physical muscles in the gym. And you will lose weight because you are controlling how you behave.

The emotional powers we need to attract money are the same forces we exercise when we want to lose weight, learn a new skill, or get that promotion we want at work. I call them the spectrum of attraction. These emotions, imagination, desire, willpower and expectation will enable us to attract money as easily as they help us to lose weight, if we learn how to improve them in our everyday life. And we will be amazed at what we can achieve. We can create the world we live in. It is down to us.

IMAGINATION

The spectrum of attraction starts with our imagination. With imagination, anything is possible. To attract the financial success and prosperity we desire, we have to imagine our life with this already in it.

We always used our imagination as children. We imagined we were astronauts and flew to the moon every day. We built dens in our gardens and imagined we were spies and superheroes. We had all these imaginary powers. There was no limit to what we could do. Our dreams were big, and we lived them in our minds. The world around us was too small to contain all we imagined we could achieve.

And then we got to school, and our dreams were tempered. Our imagination was suppressed and not supported anymore. This is not a criticism of our teachers, for the educational system is designed to allow every child the opportunity to maximise their ability. But doing so focuses on what we can do, not what we could do.

When I was at school, I wanted to be a writer. I wanted to be a writer from the day I learned to read and write. At primary school, that dream was encouraged, my imagination was allowed free rein to run wild, and I won awards for my stories. I flourished at primary school and was seen as gifted.

And yet, in secondary school, I struggled because imagination was seen as a curse, not a blessing. Those of us who tried to cling to our dreams were seen as daydreamers who didn't live in the real world and had a limited attention span. The focus was on exams, maths and science and the meanings behind words instead of the words themselves. We were told to focus, and so most of us did. We conformed to the world's expectations of us and, consequently, started to live the life we were expected to live, not the life we wanted to live.

We still use our imagination, but unfortunately, most people now use it in the wrong direction. Imagination has become a negative emotion as we imagine everything that could go wrong. If we give up our job to pursue our dreams, we imagine losing our house. If we start a business, we are scared it will take all our time and our partner will leave us. If we travel the world, we worry we may get hijacked or murdered on some lonely road in the middle of nowhere. If we write a book, we believe that nobody will buy it. Our imagination now is consumed with worry, fear and anxiety rather than hope, excitement and optimism.

Everything in this world was created twice, firstly in our minds and then in reality. If we focus on what we can't do, then we won't do it. Suppose we imagine everything that can go wrong. In that case, it will go wrong because we are attracting all those negative emotions to us. Let's go back to thinking like a child, imagining what we want with optimism and positivity. We will be giving a clear message to the Universe that is what we want. And we will attract it.

There are no limits to what we can achieve. The only limits are the ones we allow to fester in our minds. Sit for a moment now. Put this book down. Imagine what your life is like with an abundant flow of money constantly streaming towards you. The house you can live in, the car you can drive, the lifestyle you can enjoy. A life free from worry. If you can see it in your mind, you have achieved the first step to living an abundant life.

Desire

When our conscious mind is in harmony with our subconsciousness, our body will create a positive vibration. Desire is taking the vision we have originated, holding it in our consciousness and feeding it. For anything to grow and expand, it has to be fed. A flower needs water. A business requires investment. The mind is no different. It needs love. To attract money like a magnet, we need to desire a flow of abundance. Focus on it to the exclusion of all else.

Imagine for a moment that you are saving for a wedding. You are marrying the love of your life, and know exactly the type of wedding you want. You have a vision in your mind of arriving at the church in a horse-drawn carriage. The church will be filled with flowers. Flower girls dressed in pink will throw petals at your feet as you walk down the aisle. After the wedding, you and a hundred guests will drink champagne and feast on lobster and caviar in a castle overlooking a lake.

It's a beautiful vision and one that you have set your heart on. But there is one problem. It will cost a lot of money, much more than you have in your bank account now. And so, you start to save. You put money away every month and make sacrifices to enable you to have your dream wedding. Every month when you get paid, you feed your bank account and, month by month, the balance grows until you have enough to afford the wedding of your dreams.

Your dreams also need to be fed. In the same way you would feed a bank account to afford what you want or feed your body with healthy food to get the body you desire, you have to feed your dreams with thoughts to turn them into reality. Positive thoughts. Your thoughts give energy and power to that which you desire. They will connect you to what you want.

Remember that what you want already exists on some level. You can imagine it in your mind. In feeding it with desire, you are now allowing what you have created to grow. Your desire is proof that the abundance and prosperity you seek are already there for you. In the same way that if you are saving, the figures at the bottom of your bank statement show that your bank balance is growing, or if you are losing weight, the figures on the scales show that your weight is dropping, then you only have to believe that what you want will come to you. As it grows, the ideas and thoughts begin to turn into reality.

But it does not happen overnight. And unrealistic expectations can derail our dreams at this point if we let them. This mid-point in the spectrum of attraction is where many people can fail if they give up. Because in the same way, we can take the money from our bank account and treat ourselves to a spa day if the balance is not growing as quickly as we like, or splurge on a pizza if we are not losing as much weight as we want, then our desire can turn to hate if we are not manifesting prosperity in the timeframe that we expect.

This leads us onto the third stage of the spectrum of attraction.

WILLPOWER

Willpower is a potent emotion. Many people think that willpower is a force that some people have, and others don't. In reality, it is an emotion we can all use and demonstrate, providing we train our minds. And the beauty of willpower is that the more we focus on it, the easier it becomes.

Willpower is the ability to focus on one aspect of our life with all our energy. When we harness our will in the direction of our dreams, we will see amazing results. When we concentrate on what we want more than anything else, we will create a strong energy field around us that attracts what we desire. I'm not pretending it is easy to attain that level of focus and attention, but those who can achieve more than they thought possible. If they can do it, so can you. There are examples all around us. The friend who lost six stone in weight over a year. The family member who went from couch potato to endurance runner because they enrolled for a marathon. The neighbour who went from stay-at-home mum to successful business owner by turning a hobby into a business.

We can decide where we want to focus and let other ideas flow by. We can be in a challenging situation and say that enough is enough. When something goes wrong in our life, as it does to some degree or another for everybody every day, we can choose between believing that the world is against us or shrug it off. We have the freedom to focus our attention on what is good or what is bad, what is positive or that which is negative. Where we focus our thoughts is down to you. We don't lose six stone by negatively thinking we have 84lbs to lose today, but by focusing on losing half a pound every day. I would never have written a book, let alone over thirty, if I didn't sit down every day and write at least 500 words.

We can achieve whatever we want and attract an abundant flow of money, but we have to concentrate on it every day. We have the dream, know what it feels like, but we have to focus on it and want it. Hold that dream in our mind every day. Consciously control our mental powers in the direction of our desired goal. A runner cannot run a marathon unless they train most days. A person will never lose a significant amount of weight if they diet one day and don't bother the next. And we will not attract the stream of money we want to our life unless we focus our thoughts on that every day. But focus, and we will see how the energy around us shifts and changes.

EXPECTATION

The final step in the spectrum of attraction is expectation. We must train our minds to expect what we are focusing on. If we do not expect to attract an abundant flow of abundance to our life, then we will never attract it because we are giving mixed messages to the Universe.

I live on the beautiful island of Jersey and often like to spend my free time walking on the beach when the tide is out. I park my car in the harbour and often see the local fishermen either sailing out to sea with fishing rods or returning with crates full of mackerel or lobster. The sea is wild and dangerous, especially around Jersey, where the currents are strong and there are many rocks. They are putting themselves in harm's way every day of their working lives, and they are doing it because they expect to catch fish. They set off every day expecting to catch fish, and they return after each trip with a large haul.

When we want to attract something to our life, we have to expect to receive it. If we smile and say hello to someone in a store, we expect them to smile and say hello back. Most times, they will because that is how life works. Occasionally, they won't, perhaps because they are distracted, have had a bad day, or have not heard you. And when that happens, we have a choice when we go into the store again.

We can smile and say hello again, expecting they will smile and say hello back. And the chances are they will, and we will have a good shopping experience. Or we can ignore them, believe they are rude and grumpy and are not worth wasting our energy on. And they, in turn, will think us rude and moody and not worth wasting their energy on, and we have a negative experience. We do not enjoy our time in the shop and leave frustrated, angry and disappointed.

If we expect positive experiences to happen to us, they will, nine times out of ten. If we allow the one negative experience out of every ten to cast a cloud over our life, we will experience a life filled with disappointment. If we want to attract money to our lives and live our version of the dream, then we have to expect that we will when the Universe decides the time is right.

The Spectrum of Attraction

Imagine your ideal life. Bring that picture to mind. Perceive yourself living a life where you have everything you want or need. You feel happy, joyous and at peace because you have the freedom to do what you want and the opportunity to make your own decisions. Everything you wanted and imagined has been manifested, and your dream is now a reality. Say hello to your future self. They are not far away. You know what you have to do to meet them.

The life that you want is already created in your mind. Everything is there, waiting for you. You just have to want enough to reach out and get it. The only thing stopping you is you.

BELIEF

In the province of the mind, what one believes to be true either is true or becomes true. —John Lilly

As we have already seen, we attract what we give out. If we think positive thoughts, then we experience good fortune and positivity. If we think negative thoughts, then we receive poor experiences and disappointments. It is a fundamental universal law that we receive what we believe we will get.

Every moment, consciously or unconsciously, we serve as human magnets giving out our feelings and ideas and collecting more of what we've already given out. Even though we may believe we are optimistic, it is amazing how much we can allow negativity to creep into our lives.

If you don't believe me, spend a day in heightened awareness. Take notice of your negative thoughts and make a mental note. You will be surprised at how much negativity you live with. It can start when the alarm wakes you earlier than you wanted it to, you feel disgruntled that you have to get out of bed, or you wish you didn't have to go to work. You pad downstairs, knowing those who have used the kitchen before you haven't put their dirty pots away. You look out the window expecting a grey, overcast day. You get into your car knowing that the traffic will be bad, walk into work wishing it was five o'clock and time to go home, open your emails knowing there is going to be a long list of requests, and answer your mobile expecting someone to want something from you. And the list goes on and on and on. One negative thought after another until you get into bed at the end of the day worn out, weary and frustrated at the trials and tribulations of the day and expecting more of the same tomorrow. If we believe we will have a bad day, we invariably do.

And yet it doesn't have to be like that. We can change our beliefs and turn our negative thoughts into positive ones if we raise our awareness to recognise the thought and take action to stop them from taking hold in our minds. It takes knowledge and practice, but our negative thoughts are habits, and any habit can be changed. And the more we focus and practice, the more we will find that abundance and good fortune enter our lives. When we believe that life will turn out good, it usually does.

If we find ourselves mentally complaining when the alarm clock wakes us, stop the negative thought in its tracks by telling ourselves that we will have a good day. Rather than despairing when we see the dirty cups and bowls on the countertop, celebrate how clean the kitchen looks when we have stacked them in the dishwasher. Rather than opening the curtains and expecting to see a cloudy overcast day, look out the window with an open mind and find something positive to think about, whatever the weather. Instead of telling yourself that you will be stuck in traffic, see the traffic flowing freely, believe that the traffic will be light and find yourself navigating your journey with ease.

When I give that last example in the workshops I run, people tend to look at me incredulously, but you will be amazed at how powerful your thoughts can be. When I first came across these techniques, I lived in Central London and parking on the road outside my flat was a nightmare. I had acquired the belief that I would never be able to find a parking space near the flat, and I never could. But when I changed my beliefs and got close to my flat and started to tell myself that I would be able to park, something astounding happened. I could. I never again had to park in the local multi-storey or five streets away. I always found a space relatively easily. I believed I would be able to park, and the Universe delivered.

Limiting Beliefs

The way we think about money is our money mindset. We must believe that we have total control over how and when we attract it and what we do with it. Most people do not believe that. They think that the money they receive is controlled by someone or something else, a partner, an employer, the situation and the circumstances they find themselves in. And when they have received it, their responsibilities control what they do with it. And because they believe that control does not sit with them, they have a negative perspective of money. Not a positive one.

To be a money magnet, we have to overcome the beliefs that we are not in control because we are not going to attract something to which we have a negative attitude. To change our beliefs, we must clear our minds of limiting beliefs that stop us from attracting money to our lives. Maintaining positive beliefs is critical for success and wealth in our life.

What we believe about money impacts whether or not we will receive it. If we think that we have not done anything to deserve it, have not earned it, or are not clever enough to make it, then that is the message we give to the Universe. The Universe will not provide because we subconsciously say we do not believe we should have money.

Here are the commonly held limiting beliefs that will block money from flowing our way

We don't work hard enough.

In life, there are so many pressures on our time. We may have a job that takes a large proportion of our time, but we have other responsibilities too. We need to care for our bodies which may mean we go to the gym, for a jog, or a walk. We need to look after our minds, so it is essential to take some downtime, sit quietly in the garden, devote time to a hobby, or just read or watch television. We may have a family to look after, children who need feeding or ferrying from place to place, or elderly parents we need to call on. All of these responsibilities take time away from work, and we are programmed to believe that to earn money, we have to be a workaholic.

How often do we hear someone rich say they are wealthy because they sacrificed their personal life to spend every waking minute at work? Countless times, but that doesn't mean for us to be rich, we have to do the same.

Effort does not equal reward. If it did, we would all earn the same amount of money for one hour's work regardless of our work. A nurse working twelve hours a day would earn twelve times as much as an influencer spending one hour a day posting content on social media. A plumber would make the same as a footballer and a teacher as a financial trader. In a cleaning company, who works harder, the owner of the company or the people who clean? The owner has pressures; they have to get the contracts and have a responsibility to the clients and the people who work for them, but the cleaners work the hardest. And get paid the least.

The belief that only those who work hard, make sacrifices, and spend their life at work are the only people who can be rich, limits those of us who want a balanced life to believe that we will never be rich. And if we think that, then we won't be rich. Not because we don't deserve to be wealthy, but because we don't believe we deserve to be wealthy. We are subconsciously limiting our desire.

MONEY IS A LIMITED RESOURCE; TO BE RICH, YOU HAVE TO BE SELFISH.

This is very similar to the belief above, but the difference here is that there is an assumption that money is a limited resource, and therefore if we have more, then it means that others have less. Taking more than we need means being unfair to others. To keep wanting more if we don't need it is selfish.

Money is not a finite resource. There is not a mythical sack of money somewhere that, when emptied, means there is no more. If we have more than we need, it does not mean that others have less. We have not taken it out of the pockets of someone else. Others will not go without because we have a lot. Money is infinite, we can all have as much as we want and like.

IT IS EMBARRASSING TO BE RICH WHEN SO MANY ARE NOT.

Although we all need and want money, nice people don't talk about it. Or that's the common consensus anyway. Those who flaunt their wealth by driving expensive cars, wearing designer clothes and talking about how many pairs of shoes they have in their closet are considered not classy. Money is something to hide. For many, it is something that we feel guilty about. We don't like to mention how much something has cost or how much money we have. And because we see it as embarrassing, sordid even, we subconsciously repel it from our lives. If we are going to feel guilty about having money, we are pushing it away, telling the Universe to not send it in our direction. If we want to attract money, we must enjoy it, and if we want it, we must like it.

NOTHING COMES WITHOUT A PRICE.

This is the belief that with money, there is always a catch. If we have money, the Universe will extract payment in another area of our life. We need to bust that myth right now. The Universe is kind and benevolent to those who respect it. We do not have to pay the price for its gifts.

How often have we read that a lottery winner wishes they had never won the lottery because it disrupted their lives in ways they didn't want? It wrecked their marriage, damaged their relationship with their family and friends, and their life spiralled into drink or drugs. Looking back, they rued the day that their numbers came up. But it is not money that led to that, but their behaviour when they received it. They were unprepared for it, did not expect it, and no matter how much support they received, they could not handle it. Deep down, they had a limiting belief about money, that they were not worthy, had done nothing to deserve it, and felt embarrassed about what they had compared to their friends. And subconsciously threw the opportunity away.

We look at the wealthy business owner down the road whose partner has left them and think that money cannot buy love and happiness. This is true because how we behave attracts love and happiness. But on the flip side, it is not money that creates heartbreak and disappointment, but our behaviours. Whilst the Universe will always provide what we ask, it does not hold our hand or coach us in how we deal with it. That is down to us.

Living in the Past

What we want, we can see in our minds. But we can't yet experience it because although the reality is in our minds, it has not yet manifested itself into our physical world. We are taking the steps towards our targets but have not yet reached them. And if we are unwary, there is something very simple and easy to do that can derail us. And that is if we slip into living in the past.

We have all been on a journey that has brought us to where we are now. And as you have picked up this book, the chances are that that journey has been challenging, difficult, and strewn with obstacles. What you may have wanted has not manifested itself in your lives. You are not as far along the path as you would have liked. You may have found yourselves in a different place from where you expected to be.

If that is the case, it is very easy to focus on the past. But if you want to move forward, you must stop looking back, however hard this may be for you. You cannot move ahead if you spend your time focusing on the past. What has happened has happened. It cannot be changed. The past has gone, and although you may be living now with the decisions you made and the experiences and events that occurred, you cannot waste a second thinking about them.

It is not easy to forget the past, but if we want to create a better tomorrow, a future filled with wealth and abundance, then we have to. We cannot change our past. We can only shape our future. If someone has hurt us deeply, we must accept it and move on. If we have experienced bad luck, we must shrug our shoulders and believe that good fortune will appear. If we have lost everything, we must trust that we do not need it because the Universe will provide more than we need or want. By living in the past, we are giving it a relevance, when it has no relevance. It is gone. All that matters is now and from this day forward.

Louise Hay, the founder of Hay House and probably one of the most successful and well-known authors of new thought, was raped at the age of 5, dropped out of school at the age of 15 and worked in a succession of low-paid jobs before writing "You Can Heal Your Life", one of the world's best-selling advice books at the age of 58. JK Rowling was an impoverished single mother writing in her spare time whose Harry Potter books were rejected over and over again before the rights were finally bought, and she became one of the richest authors of all time. Oprah Winfrey was fired from her first job in TV. Steven Spielberg was rejected twice into the University of Southern California's School of Cinematic Arts. If they had believed that their past would influence their future, they would never have achieved what they did. The past no longer exists. It is gone. If you do just one thing today, let this be it. Make a commitment to yourself from this second that you will live only in the now and focus on the future. And close the door on your past once and for all.

Positive Money Affirmations

Limiting beliefs can be deep-rooted. They are so deeply embedded in our subconscious that we may not even know we have them. The simplest way to shift these beliefs and change our life is to start to state positive money affirmations. Affirmations are positive statements to encourage us to visualise a future of abundance and wealth through simple thoughts said repeatedly. These can be written down, or we can display something that will make us remember. If you are writing them down, write them on pieces of paper and display them around your home, your car, or your workstation at work. If you are using something as a reminder, anything personal can be used. I always carry crystals, one in my pocket and one on a chain around my neck. When I touch the crystal, it reminds me to speak a positive affirmation out loud. Excellent crystals for wealth are Citrine and Carnelian. I have a picture in my bedroom representing wealth; when I look at it, I recite a specific positive affirmation. I also have a room mist by the side of my bed representing confidence and self-esteem and spray it each morning whilst repeating a positive affirmation. It doesn't matter what you use, just that it has a special meaning to you.

When practised regularly, affirmations can improve our self-worth by reflecting internally on our core values. Positive affirmations are personal to each of us. In this book, the focus is on money and attracting wealth, prosperity and abundance to our lives, but positive affirmations can help us attract anything we want. Below I have given you some examples of positive affirmations you can say as often as you want daily.

I live a life of infinite financial abundance.
Prosperity and wealth are an integral part of my life.
I accept and welcome financial success.
New income channels will flow into my life effortlessly
I trust my judgment to make sound financial decisions.
Money is drawn to me, and I am drawn to it.
I attract money easily.
I am perceptive of opportunities that will make me money.
I am worthy of having money.
I am a strong money magnet.
I will always have enough money for what I want to do.
I will find money in expected and unexpected ways.
My life is rich and full of abundance
My money helps change the world for the better.
I am allowed to have success and happiness.
My money will do good for the people I love.

VISION

One's vision is not a road map but a compass. —Peter Block

Once we start changing our thinking, it is as though we have opened our minds to all the possibilities in the world. We can see them with our own eyes. We may not be living our dream yet, but we can see it as clearly as if we are, feel it, touch it. Once implanted in our minds, those ideas and thoughts are allowed to take root, spread and grow, like a seed grabbed by the wind and scattered on the earth. To see our new, wonderful, abundant life in our mind is the first small step we take to build it in our reality.

If we were to diet, if we want to lose weight and get the beach body we desire in preparation for our holiday in a few months, then the common wisdom is that we need to change our approach to the food we eat. We need to alter our whole relationship with food, eat a more balanced diet with plenty of fruits, vegetables and grains, reduce our reliance on food that is full of fats and sugar, eat smaller amounts more often, and take the time to enjoy our food, creating an event out of a meal as opposed to eating on the go. And yet most people, when they are dieting, restrict the types of foods they eat, count calories and fast for long periods.

These diets can work and are likely to give you the beach body you desire for your next holiday, but by following a diet like that, you are not changing your life, attitude or long-term behaviour. The chances are that during your holiday, you would start to pile on the pounds and, within a few months of that holiday, have put any weight you had lost back on. Because you had placed restrictions on yourself, you had taken something away, and as soon as you had got what you desired, you felt free to go back to what you wanted to do. Your focus with these diets is the diet itself and not the reason you are dieting. You are, in effect, creating short-term pain for short-term gain. But what if you were to alter your thinking and, instead of focusing on your diet, focused on being healthy.

If every day, when we looked in the mirror, we saw our future self rather than our current self, we would have created our future reality in our mind. If you see yourself on holiday sitting at a beachfront table in a beautiful white sarong, eating a wholesome salad of freshly bought vegetables and locally caught seafood, drinking a glass of sparkling water, a glass of champagne at your side, your current self will automatically make the choices your future self needs. If you are eating a salad in your mind, you will not eat a pizza in your reality. If your future self is nibbling on an apple, your current self will not raid the biscuit tin. In creating your future life in your head, your brain takes the actions now that will help you to achieve it. And in a few months, you will discover that you can fit in the bikini you bought without even trying. There does not need to be any pain for long-term gain.

We already have our vision. We already know what we want our future life to look like. We have built the abundant life that we want in our mind. Now we have found and discovered it, we need to ensure that we focus on it. All the things that we focus on will be created. It does not matter whether it is an image we want. If we focus on our weight and see ourself as fat and overweight, that is what we will remain because that is what we will attract. If we see yourself as poor, struggling to make ends meet daily, that is what we will stay. No matter our current circumstances, if we want our future situation to be different, we must build our future life in our minds. An architect knows what a new house looks like before it is built. A fashion designer knows what a dress looks like before it is made. Building or creating our future is no different. First of all, it is designed in our mind.

First, we must form a clear and defined mental picture of what we want. In doing this, we must not think about vague ideas or concepts but be specific and describe every detail of our vision. Write it down and explain all the details we can see with our minds. We do not need to think about how we will achieve it because it is not important at this stage how it will be achieved. When we place an order in a restaurant for a meal, we are not telling the chef how to cook it. We trust that the chef will cook it how we want. When we take an aeroplane to a destination, we do not check the route with the pilot. We expect the pilot to have studied the way and will take us where we want to go. It is the same when we order an abundant and prosperous life from the Universe. It is enough to expect it. We do not need to give the Universe directions on providing it.

The next step is to create a vision board. Take a square piece of cardboard and spend half a day filling it with pictures representing the life you want. The house that you want to live in. The car that you want to drive. Photographs of destinations that you want to visit. These are examples for I cannot tell you what to include because it is personal to you. Whatever your future, perfect, ideal life looks like, create a pictorial representation. And then display it somewhere in your home where you cannot fail to see it.

I created my first vision board when I was in my mid-twenties. It is fair to say that my first few years of work were not inspiring. They weren't a failure, but I achieved very little in the first eight years of my career. I was doing the same job, at pretty much the same salary, as I had when I started work. As my peers and friends got promoted, increased wages, bought houses, new cars, and built relationships, I plodded along, still living with my parents at home because I couldn't afford to move out, still single because I couldn't afford to date.

I don't know what the catalyst was for me. It could have been a book, a magazine article, or perhaps something I watched on the TV, but one day I decided to create a vision board. I cut pictures out of magazines of a sports car and a beautiful house overlooking a lake. I cut out a picture of a book and a pen representing my dream to be a writer, a map of

Manhattan, a place I had always wanted to go, a horse, for one of my dreams was to own a racehorse, and pictures of stacks of money. And when I had finished sticking the images to my vision board, I placed it on the back of my bedroom door, where I would see it every day

Within a year, I had moved out of my parent's home into a new build on a small executive cul-de-sac, although it would be another 13 years before I lived in a large farmhouse overlooking a lake. It took three years before I was driving a sports car and four years before I visited New York travelling business class. My first book was published in 2012, and I have now written 36 books, 37 including this one, although they are not all under my name because they are in different genre. The first vision board is long gone, thrown away accidentally in a move, but I can still see it in my mind when I think back, and I have achieved most of what was on there. I now have a new vision board and every expectation that I will achieve my dreams because when we focus on them, the Universe provides.

This brings me to the next step, focusing on your vision frequently. When you do, you should be calm and let your intuition take over. Now is the time to be still, to let the idea be implanted firmly in your mind. Take possession of it, own it. It is yours and yours alone. The time for action is soon, but not now. If we try to run without having planted the destination in our mind, then we are doomed to failure.

This is where most people go wrong. We are programmed to succeed through hard work, being busy, faking it until we make it and forcing change through. People are constantly trying to make things happen how they want them to. And they may succeed partially. But the problem is if we have told the Universe what we want, we need to give the Universe the time to work its magic. To force the change through ourselves is like hiring a wedding planner to create our dream wedding and then doing everything ourselves. We will get a wedding that is at the limit of our imagination, but we are unlikely to be truly satisfied with what we have achieved.

The final step is to trust. The Universe has its own timetable. No one can tell us how long it will take to see our dreams become a reality. But believe that although we cannot see it manifest in our physical world, it is there, taking seed, beginning to grow.

BEHAVIOURS

Behaviour is the mirror in which we can display our image. —Mahatma Gandhi

We will naturally invite positive things into our life if we concentrate our energy on what we want and what we have. However, the danger that most of us fall into is that we spend most of our time focusing on what we don't have. We feel down because we don't have enough money. We see an Instagram post of a celebrity on holiday and wish we had their freedom. We feel sad, let down, disappointed, and discouraged with our lot in life. And as a consequence, we invite more of the same.

It is a universal law that focusing negatively on what we don't have will attract more disappointment and negativity into our life. If we focus on what we have, we will attract more happiness and positivity into our life. Negativity brings more negativity. Positivity brings more positivity. It is a simple fact. If we wake up in the morning full of energy, smiling at the world as we throw open our curtains, then the chances are that we will have a good day. If we wake to scowl at the alarm clock, throwing off the bedcovers in a temper before stomping into the bathroom, we will probably not have a great day, no matter what happens to us.

A friend once told me that people were naturally drawn to me. It was said after we had spent a couple of hours shopping and then had an early dinner in a restaurant. My friend commented that we had had conversations with pretty much everyone we had come into contact with in the shops and got a complimentary glass of sparkling wine from the waiter in the restaurant whilst we had been choosing our meal.

There is truth in what she said, people are naturally drawn to me, but that is because I view strangers as friends I have not yet had the pleasure of meeting. I smile at shop assistants, talk to them, laugh with them, and they respond with the same. Even an arduous task like grocery shopping can be viewed positively or negatively. If you approach it positively and believe you will enjoy the experience, you will.

Positivity attracts positivity. I know I have written that only a few sentences ago, but I cannot stress it too many times. If you smile at someone, they will smile back. If you talk to someone, they will talk back. If you expect something good to happen to you, then it will. It may not be what you expected, but you will receive a gift from the Universe. And if you think positively about money, you will attract more of it into your life.

Negativity attracts negativity. If you scowl at someone, they will frown back. If you ignore the person sitting next to you on the train, they will ignore you. If you expect something bad to happen, your fears will likely be realised. And if you think negatively about money, and believe you will never have enough for your needs, let alone your desires, then guess what? You won't.

Demonstrating positive behaviours is far more than constantly smiling and talking to people as we do our daily business. It is about keeping a strong positive outlook even when everything seems to fall apart. If we nourish our minds with happy thoughts, even in the face of adversity, we will see incredible changes in our surroundings. If we begin to think positively, we perceive the world differently. We will be in total control of our thoughts and find a solution to every problem.

In many respects having a positive attitude can be advantageous. So how can we programme our thoughts to create a positive mental mindset?

Be Optimistic

It is well recognised that happiness is linked to a positive mental mindset. Happiness is a mental state that comes from inside, and although it is connected to external factors, it is an emotion that is not controlled by external factors. Although we do not always have control over what happens to us, we have total control over how we react to those events.

We all know of glass-half-full types, people who keep smiling no matter what disasters befall them. They could lose the roof over their head and still feel the joy of having the sun on their face. We also know people who are glass-half-empty types, those who find a penny and lament the fact that they didn't find a pound. If we want to attract money into our lives, we have to programme our minds to believe that we will attract money into our lives, look for the benefits in any setback, and focus on what we have rather than what we don't. An optimistic mindset sees possibilities rather than problems and opportunities instead of obstacles.

Be Confident

If we believe in ourself and trust that we have the knowledge, skills and attitude to achieve whatever we want in life, we will start to attract positivity to us like a magnet. Wear what you feel good in, regardless of whatever anyone else thinks. Hold your head high. Speak with authority. We are unique individuals with exceptional talents, and rather than trying to hide for fear of bringing attention to ourselves, we should project ourselves out to the Universe. To attract money, we must first attract the Universe's attention. Nobody can do that for us. We need to do it ourselves.

Be Healthy

Health can positively impact wealth if we maintain a healthy body and mind. We should always strive to keep our body healthy, eat a balanced diet with fresh produce, drink in moderation, have a regular pamper session, and keep moving, whether at the gym or walking in the fresh air.

We also need to look after our minds, set ourselves a challenge and goal, be inquisitive, constantly ask questions, and search for answers. Life is for living. One of my favourite quotes is that there is no point in living if you don't feel alive.

To attract money, we must look good, feel good and be good. If we have looked after our bodies and treated them with the reverence and care they deserve, they will look after us. If we feel good, then we will automatically look good. If we know that we look good, that confidence will shine through in our faces. We have complete control over our behaviours. We have the power to influence how we look and feel. If we make the most of what life has given us, the Universe will ensure that we receive more of all it has to offer.

ACTIONS

When you do the things in the present that you can see, you are shaping the future that you are yet to see. —Idowu Koyenikan

We must now connect our newly acquired way of thinking with personal action. This is where many people fail, believing that money will magically appear immediately if they think about it. And when it doesn't, when a couple of days have passed, and they haven't seen any material difference, they decide that it doesn't work and so give up and, in the process, miss out.

We have to back our change of mindset with action. If the Universe is going to help us, we must first help ourselves. It is the same process we go through when we want to change our life. If we decide to lose weight, we have to change our attitude toward food and then take action to buy healthier products and put smaller portions on our plates. If we decide to raise our self-esteem, we must first change our image in our minds and then portray that to the outer world. And if we have decided that we will be rich, we must create that reality in our minds before taking action to bring that reality into the present. It is not enough to sit back and do nothing. Without activity, the reality in our mind shifts and becomes only a dream.

The first step is always the hardest, but it is the most important. The first step sets us in our direction of travel. We may hesitate either through fear of failure or even success. We may tell ourselves that what we know is safe, and what is unknown may not hold the same security or comfort. We may question the wisdom of taking the first step when we don't know where the following steps will lead. What is important is that we act now. If we wait, we may not begin.

So, what are the actions that we need to take? Only you know that because only you know what your future reality looks like. It would be remiss of me to offer no suggestions, though, so I've included a few here to give you some examples. They are all small, easy actions that you can take. They range from the mundane to the metaphysical. They are not exhaustive and are certainly not written here to be followed to the letter, for the action itself is less important than the act of taking action.

Dress to Impress

Start to dress as though you are rich. Wear bold, powerful colours like red, purple and gold, all colours that unsurprisingly are associated with wealth. If you dress well, you are likely to be noticed, and one of those who see you could be so impressed that they send an opportunity your way.

Utilise your skills

We all have skills and knowledge that go under-utilised because we are so busy completing the actions and responsibilities we have to others. But those skills that you have could start to earn you money. If you are good at writing, write a book and self-publish it, or write content for someone's blog. If you are creative with your hands, make something to sell online or at craft fairs. If you are good with children or animals, become a babysitter or pet sitter. The list is almost endless.

Sell unwanted items

Our lives are filled with possessions that we no longer need or use. Gather everything together that you no longer want and sell it. It is incredible how much money you can get from your unwanted clutter, for as the saying goes "one man's trash is another man's treasure".

Rent out something you don't use

In addition to possessions, you may also have space you don't need or use. That empty drive may be perfect parking for someone who works in the office down the road. Your spare room could be used as a holiday let or become a home away from home for someone who works in your local area during the week. Your garden could even be turned into an allotment for a gardener who lives in an apartment without access to outside space.

Spring clean your finances.

When was the last time you compared how much you were paying for a service with the service from another provider? You will be amazed how much you can save by taking a competitive deal with an alternative organisation. You could also check your bank statement and identify all those direct debits to ensure that you only pay for services you want or use. A few years ago, I decided to investigate what the direct debit was that I was paying £24.99 a month for and discovered that it was for a subscription that I had set up over five years before and which I had never used. It was a relatively small amount, but I had wasted £1500 over the years. Once we control and appreciate the small amounts, we signal to the Universe that we can handle more incredible wealth.

Self - Promotion

We are a reserved bunch deep down. We don't like to put ourselves out there and tell people how good we are for fear of being considered bold or over-confident. But if you are to attract money, you need to not only demonstrate to others how good you are but tell them as well.

Talk to a stranger

A few years ago, I got a contract, and a significant amount of money through a chance encounter with someone I started chatting to in a café. That person at the next table, on the seat next to you, behind you in the queue, may have a golden opportunity for you. Or maybe doing or using something that gives you the spark of an idea. Or knows someone who could help you in some way. Everyone has a story to tell and loves to tell it. Offer them the chance to talk and what they reveal could be amazing.

These are just a few ideas. There are countless more. Think about your life, what you want, and the opportunities that will come flooding in. It is less important what you do, just that you do something. Once you have taken the first step, the second step becomes more manageable, and before long, the Universe sits up and takes note.

LIMITING ACTIONS

Notice in the previous paragraph how I said that what you do is less important? There was a reason I wrote that instead of that it was not important what action you take. And that is because the action has to take you forward, not backwards.

Hold on, I hear you say. Surely all actions take us forward. If only that were true. The trap that the unwary can fall into, if they are not careful, is that they can take an action that limits their ability to attract money. In the same way that we can have limiting beliefs, we can also take limiting actions. Limiting actions deprive us of something we want, prevent us from doing something we want, or stop the flow of money into our life.

Let me give an example. We want more money in our lives and for our bank balance to grow, so we decide to save. We put every penny we do not need to spend in our bank account. We have probably all read stories of people who have managed to put down a deposit on a house because they have not eaten in a restaurant, taken a vacation, treated themselves to any new clothes, or had a haircut or manicure in the last five years. And having deprived themselves of all but the essentials they need to live, they have managed to save £30,000 and can put down a deposit on a new house.

But are they attracting a constant flow of money to their life? No, of course, they aren't. In some respect, they are stifling it because what they are saying to the Universe is that they believe that money is a finite resource and they need to save what they have because they won't receive any more.

There is a huge difference between saving what you can whilst enjoying what you have and restricting your life so that you can put money to one side. In the first action, we are saying to the Universe that we respect money and control it. We deserve more because we know how to treat it. In the second action, we are telling the Universe that money has control over us. We should only receive what we need because we are not able to utilise any more.

Let us look at other limiting actions that we can take that act as a barrier to us receiving the riches of the Universe.

Discount Shopping

Contentious, I know, because we all love a bargain, me as much as anyone. So let me clarify what I mean. I don't mean finding something that we want, need or always buy on a discount and buying it. That's a gift from the Universe and should be celebrated. Instead, I mean depriving ourselves of something we want or need that is full price and hoping that later in the year, it will be discounted. Or waiting until the last hour of the store opening hours and rooting around in the clearance bin for anything that is knocked down in price. Finding that our usual brand of coffee is full price but another brand is half price and buying the alternative to save money. Needing one item but buying two because the second item is half price and we hope it may come in useful later. If we take these limiting actions, we are stuck in a poverty mindset, believing that we always need to find an offer because we do not have enough to buy what we want at full price.

Discount shopping links to one of the limiting beliefs discussed earlier in this book. That money is a limited resource. Because we believe that money is a finite resource, that once we have spent what we have, we will not receive any more, then we conserve what we have and spread it thinly to ensure that there is enough to last. But if we believe that we are a money magnet and honestly think we can attract a limitless supply of money into our lives, then there is no need to do this. If we trust that the Universe will provide, we should buy what we want at the price we believe it is worth.

Stealing and Cheating

If I asked most people if they were a thief, they would probably say no. But the reality is somewhat different because most of us, to one degree or another, steal or cheat. Not deliberately, and certainly not to cause another person loss. But if the opportunity presents itself, those in a poverty mindset will take the chance to obtain something for nothing.

It may be the sachets of coffee and sugar or the little bottles of shampoo and conditioner for guests' use in a hotel. If we haven't used them, we think they were there for our use, so we will take them home. Or we need an envelope to send a letter to someone and haven't got one so grab one from work. It may be that we have driven to the shops and think that as we are only going to be ten minutes, we will not pay for parking, or we park in the supermarket car park even though it is only for shoppers and we are not shopping there. We may buy a train ticket for a child when our child is over 14 or fill our flask with coffee from the free refill at the café. Little things that we think nothing of but mean that someone else has lost out.

And we have lost out, too, because the message we are sending to the Universe is that we do not have enough money to buy what we want, so we have to steal it instead.

Postponement

When we take action, we expect an instant result. When we put one foot in front of another, we get somewhere. When we eat something, we feel full. When we drink something, we no longer feel thirsty. When we hand over a pound coin to buy something, we receive something in return.

When we decide to change our mindset to become more prosperous and take action to attract wealth into our life, we expect an instant response. Sometimes this happens. I met someone very recently who was going through a bad patch financially in his life and who came to me for a coaching session. Within a week of him talking to me, he had sold the business he had been trying to sell for several months, and a job he had initially been turned down three months ago was suddenly offered to him because of a change of management. More often, though, it is a slow burn. Seemingly inconsequential tiny changes happen, which we barely notice until we look back and see how our life has changed over the preceding few months. And this lack of progress can lead to us feeling despair, helpless to live the changes we want.

We feel conflicted. We have altered our mindset to try and see the positive in every situation. We have started to take better care of our body, are watching what we eat and trying to add some exercise every day. Rather than throwing on the item of clothing on the nearest hanger when we open the wardrobe door, we are taking time to match and accessorise. Our whole demeanour is one of wealth and abundance, but we do not feel wealthy. And that will risk derailing the money that is heading our way because we feel like a fraud.

When we change our outlook and mindset, the Universe does not necessarily react instantly or consistently, and certainly not always in the way we expect. You may be about to get a better-paid job, yet that vacancy has not materialised yet. You could be about to find an opportunity to create another income stream, but the stars have not yet aligned to put it in your path. You might be about to get a cashback offer from something that you bought last week, but it hasn't been processed yet. These money opportunities are heading your way, yet they have not been realised, which creates a problem. Because although you look the part, although you are behaving as though you have the wealth you desire, it has not yet manifested in your pocket, purse or bank account. You do not have what you wish at this moment in time.

We have already seen that positivity attracts positivity, and negativity attracts negativity. Money attracts money. Poverty attracts poverty. If we act as though we have nothing, then we will receive nothing, which creates a problem. How do we act rich if we do not yet have the riches we want?

There is a simple answer, which we have probably all done at some point without realising. It is called postponement. It is committing to a course of action at some point in the future and trusting that the Universe will provide when that date comes. We need to be careful here because I am not advocating buying something on a credit card because wealth and abundance are not created by buying on credit. It is making the decision now but postponing the action to a date in the future.

Postponement in Action

We have all, at one time or another, demonstrated postponement. It could be that we have booked a holiday for the summer or Christmas, and although we have not got the funds in our account right now, we believe and trust that the funds will be available once the holiday needs to be paid for. When couples plan a wedding, often a costly event, they do not necessarily have the money to pay for everything there and then and don't need to. But whether they realise it or not, they expect the Universe to deliver the funds to them so they can have the wedding of their dreams.

The same approach can be used for short-term decisions we need to make. If our friend invites us out to lunch tomorrow, and we cannot afford it and feel bad that we do not have the money to accept their invitation, the tendency is to tell our friend that we cannot afford it. We say phrases like "I can't afford to go out for lunch with you" or "I haven't got the money for lunch". Remember that we create our reality, and by saying these words, we are saying that we do not have enough to do what we want. But if we genuinely believe that the Universe will provide what we want, then rather than say we can't afford it, we can state confidently, with a smile on our face. "I can do lunch next week". We are not postponing the decision. We have decided to treat ourselves and enjoy a nice lunch with a friend. We are just delaying the action.

Now the risk is that you may worry that you won't have the money. Or mentally work out what you can scrimp on over the coming week so you can afford to go out to lunch. That is not a positive mindset because you think that to receive a treat, you have to earn it somehow. That you have to give something up to receive a reward is a limiting belief. You do not have to earn a reward. There is no balance to be maintained. The

Universe provides abundantly. You just have to believe that the Universe will provide. To create the reality that you want in your mind.

Don't postpone the decision until you have got the right situation. Do not wait for a change of environment before you act. Make the decision now to create the future position you want. Move in the direction that seems right to you. And the Universe will provide you with the tools that will help you on your way.

Momentum

Success requires first expending 10 units of effort to produce one unit of results. Your momentum will then produce 10 units of results with each unit of effort. —Charles J. Givens

Building momentum

We know from the law of physics that once an object is in motion it is easy to keep it in motion. When a child is playing on a swing, it takes effort and power to start, but once started, the child can stay swinging for a long time with barely any effort whatsoever. It is the same when we take action to attract money into our life. Although effort is needed in the beginning to take the first step, we only need a fraction of the effort to maintain it. The second, third and subsequent steps are much easier to take.

Let us take one of the examples from the list of possible actions in the previous chapter. You love animals and have decided to be a pet sitter and dog walker. You have created some flyers and posted them through the letterboxes in your neighbourhood. You have added a post to social media, so you sit back and wait for the phone to ring.

It takes a little while, but finally, you get your first client. And you take their dog for a walk. Someone sees you and asks for your number, and suddenly you have your second client. Your first client is so pleased with how happy and safe their dog was with you that they not only book you again but tell their friends. Within a week, you have your third, fourth and fifth clients, and one of them has become a regular. Another one is going on holiday in a month and asks you to pet sit for a week. Taking the first step and getting the first client felt challenging, but new clients suddenly appear daily.

When the Universe knows that you are open to attracting money to your life, it will often throw you a curve ball. Something that you were not expecting but that you need to be open to. What you will receive will not only come from one direction. Lots of opportunities will come your way from many different directions.

Let us imagine that in the week you were pet-sitting, you groomed the dog because you noticed that its fur was a little matted. Your client comes back and cannot believe how good the dog looks. She tells you that she hasn't had the chance to take the dog to be groomed because all the local groomers are booked up months in advance. A light bulb goes off in your head that this is something you could offer on a mobile basis, so you start suggesting this to your clients. Many of them are thrilled that you can provide this and book you. Even more money starts to flow towards you.

It seems that you can do no wrong; what you want just drops into your lap. You could call it chance, good fortune, or coincidence, but it is down to your mindset coupled with your actions. You have made a commitment to yourself that you will be prosperous and have taken action to make that your reality. And it is. Because of what we think we are. We create our reality. We are in control of our reality. We are our reality.

Negative momentum

Momentum works all the time and we can find ourselves moving in a negative momentum from time to time. Our actions are aligned with our thoughts, and our thoughts create our reality. So, if we think that everything is working against us, that we can't do something, that we are not getting the breaks we deserve, then that becomes our reality.

Again, using the example above, your side hustle as a pet sitter and dog walker has gone from strength to strength over the last six months. You have many clients impressed with your service and have diversified into grooming and selling pet supplies. You are making hundreds of pounds of extra income every month. The Universe then decides to send even more money your way, with yet another golden opportunity, but this time it stops you in our tracks. Because you fear that this new opportunity is too big to deal with, it will take skills and knowledge that you do not have and will take too much time. And so, say No.

By doing that, what message are we giving to the Universe? That we are not open to a limitless supply of money? That our ambitions are small, not large? That we have enough for what we want? That we have achieved the limit of our dreams? And what about the message that we are giving to ourselves? That we have grown to the maximum of our capabilities? That we do not deserve more? That we have achieved what we can? By saying no, we are raising our hand to the Universe and saying enough is enough. We do not want or deserve anymore. We are happy with what we have.

We have tried to stop the flow of money, but the momentum does not stop. We cannot stop a child on a swing in mid-swing. The momentum will just continue in the other direction. Our mindset has changed from one where we believe that the Universe supplies an endless stream of money to one in which we think we have reached the limit of our dreams. And the pendulum moves back. We lose what we have gained.

We should not fall into the trap of saying No. The Universe will show us the way if we are open to possibilities. If we look for them, the Universe will help us find the resources we need and the people who can help us. To be rich, we have to live without putting a limit on what we can achieve. We have to believe that we will find a way. Once we move in a positive direction, we must maintain that direction daily.

VALUE

The more you praise and celebrate your life, the more there is in life to celebrate. —Oprah Winfrey

If we want to be rich, we first have to value ourselves. We cannot attract wealth and prosperity if we do not value ourselves. We are sending a message to the Universe that we are not worthy, that someone else is more deserving. And we miss out and let others take what we should rightfully have.

We are unique, beautiful, and talented in our way. It does not matter what someone else thinks. All that matters is what we think and believe. There is a saying that beauty is in the eye of the beholder, but actually, our beauty is in our own eyes. If we believe that our worth and value are in the hands of others, then we pass control of our life over to them. What happens to us, what we receive, and what we are offered is always in the hands of others.

How often have you said yes to something when you wanted to say no?

Your friend asks you to go to town shopping with them, and you do it, and in the process, spend money you did not want to spend because you feel selfish if you say no. A co-worker asks you to help them with their work, and you do it even though you must stay late to finish it. Your son asks you to take him to the football match because it is raining and he doesn't want to get wet walking, and you do even though you wanted some quiet time for yourself after a busy, stressful week. We play many roles in life, friend, parent, and co-worker, but the most important one is us, the one that we are in danger of valuing the least.

This lack of self-worth can lead to others taking advantage of us deliberately or unconsciously. If we let others take advantage of us, we are telling the Universe that we allow others to take control of our actions. We are not able to think for ourselves or take action ourselves. Others should receive the gifts before us because we will let others decide what we will do with them. To receive those gifts for ourselves, we have to prove that we will decide what we will do, and the only way we can do this is by valuing ourselves above everyone else.

Whatever we like to do, want to do, need to do, we should do it. If we want time for ourselves, we should take it. If we do not want to go shopping with friends, we should say so. They are still our friends, but if they decide to take offence or umbrage, that is up to them. Because they are in control of their emotions, not you. You are responsible for your thoughts, actions, and feelings. You have no control over the thoughts, actions and feelings of those around you, even though they may want to pass them on to you.

A danger to our self-value is when we compare ourselves to others. We look at others and think they are happier, richer, slimmer, more attractive, and luckier than us. And so, our self-value and self-worth reduce. We should never compare ourselves to others. We are unique and perfect as we are. At this moment, we are who we should be. Comparing ourselves to others leads to envy and worry. Emotions that can derail the positive mindset we need to have if we are to attract money to our life

If we are envious of others, we signal others are more deserving than us, and we will never have what we want or deserve. If we worry, our focus is on what we don't have rather than what we do. Envy and worry create more hardship for ourselves. They are negative emotions that reduce our self-worth.

Alignment

The Universe is not punishing you. It is not blessing you. It is not controlling you. It is responding to your vibration. Think happy, and happiness will come to you. Think negatively and negativity will come to you. What we put out into the Universe we get back like an echo.
—Abraham Hicks

We have spent most of this book focusing on our internal energies and how we can change our mindset to attract money into our life. In this penultimate chapter, I will show you how your external environment can hugely impact your internal energies, boosting your life in ways you cannot even imagine.

Feng Shui is an ancient Chinese system which seeks to balance opposites in all aspects of our environment to create positive energy. By implementing the principles of Feng Shui in our homes, we can help balance and align the positive energy in our environment with our internal energies to bring good fortune, wealth and abundance to our lives. Once the flow of internal positive energy in our minds is aligned with a positive flow of energy in our home, it has the same effect on our lives as a turbo has on an engine. It brings greater power and focus, supporting us to receive whatever we want in life quicker and more efficiently.

I have been a Feng Shui practitioner and follower for over twenty years. Feng Shui is often misunderstood and made more complicated than it is, and I have spent a large part of the last 20 years demystifying it in the training courses that I have delivered. Many superstitions have grown around Feng Shui and many different schools of thought, which often means practitioners give conflicting advice. If we cut through all that, the foundation stones of good Feng Shui, the two absolutes we must get right if we are to attract good fortune to our home and what we desire in our life, are balance and energy flow.

When creating balance, it is important to understand the difference between yin and yang. In Yin Yang theory, everything in the Universe comprises opposite but interconnected forces. These opposite but interconnected forces constantly move in a cycle together through the Universe. They are dependent on one another for their very existence. When one is at its peak, the other one begins.

The best way to describe the movement of yin and yang is to look for examples in the world around us. When a tree is laden with fruit, the fruit drops to the ground spilling its seeds onto the ground to self-pollinate. When the days reach their longest in the height of summer, the next day, the days start to draw in as we start the cycle towards winter. We grow through adolescence to reach our physical peak in mid-life before old age slows us down and death moves us on to the next stage. Yin and yang are both necessary. Without seeds from the fruit, nothing else can grow. If winter didn't follow summer, we would have a hot, barren world. If summer didn't follow winter, the land would be like the frozen landscape of the arctic.

For our home to be balanced so that energy works in harmony with ourselves to attract what we desire to our lives, we need to ensure both yin and yang are equally represented in our homes. Yin is passive, dark, cold, and quiet. Yang is active, light, sunny and noisy. Yin is like autumn and winter. Yang is like spring and summer. Applying the principles to our home will help us bring balance to our environment, aiding the natural flow of energy and producing positive energy around us. A home that is too full of yin can block the natural flow of energy and allow it to stagnate. A home that is too yang disrupts the natural flow of energy, making it move too fast. Applying the principles of yin yang theory and Feng Shui helps us to harmonize our environment, bringing everything together to support us in attaining our dreams.

If we now turn our attention to energy, this flows through the Universe, our world, our immediate environment and within and around ourselves in a constant wave. It enters our homes and bodies and gives us the essence of being, the sense of feeling alive. Because it is a constant flow, it brings about change. Every minute of every day, our environment, the world and the Universe are changing. Although we may feel the same, we are completely different from the person we were before. Without energy, we would stagnate and stay the same, so we must do what we can to support the natural flow of energy.

We try our best to maintain healthy energy by exercising, eating healthy food, drinking plenty of fluids and keeping our minds active and mentally stimulated. By eating a balanced diet, being physically and mentally active and living as generous and giving life as we can, we help to support the movement of energy through our body in a natural flowing way.

In the same way that we keep our bodies healthy by eating a balanced diet and looking after our physical well-being, we need to ensure that the energy in our home is kept healthy. On a basic level, this means that our home needs to be kept clean and in good repair, rooms kept tidy and free of clutter and interiors decorated beautifully and stylishly. On a more advanced level, we can harmonize and balance energy in our homes to promote positive energy by using Feng Shui.

By using Feng Shui to balance our environment, we can help to ensure that the changes in our lives are positive and we attract what we desire. As we are not the same person we were before, we can decide who we will be in the future. Our hopes and dreams can be realized if we believe and trust in the powerful energy force that surrounds us and nurtures it as it flows through ourselves and our environment. In the following pages, I will provide some easy-to-follow tips that you can start to utilize straight away.

The Front of Your Home

If the front of your house is the face of your home, then your front door is one of the most critical elements in Feng Shui. As well as being the entrance to your home, it also acts as the mouth of your home where positive energy enters. Make sure that the doorway is kept in good repair. Doors should be regularly varnished or painted, and hinges should be well-oiled, so they don't squeak. Solid doors are better than doors with glass. If you have a glass door, the glass should be kept clean and consider covering the inside of the door with a thick curtain to ensure that energy, once it has entered, is kept within the home.

To attract good fortune to your home, consider painting your front door an auspicious colour. The Chinese believe that red is the best colour for a door, but this is only true if the front door of your home faces south. If your front door faces east, green is an excellent colour as this will signify new growth and opportunities. If your front door faces north, paint it black or dark blue, as this will help attract money and new work opportunities to the home. Finally, yellow is the most auspicious colour of all as this will help to attract luck, good fortune and abundance.

If you have a path to your door, it is best if it is wide enough for two people to walk side by side. This should be distinct from any driveway or pathway that runs past your home. If this is not possible, for example, if your doorway opens direct from the pavement or street, then try and create a barrier of some sort; small bushes planted at either side of the entrance, hanging baskets filled with flowers, or a row of multi-coloured pebbles in front of the door all work. If you do have a path, it is best if this allows energy to meander to your door rather than travel in a straight line. Again, you can create the illusion of a winding path by planting shrubs, using different coloured paving, or creating different surfaces using a mix of stones, slabs, and grass. Keep your path clean, neat and clear of any obstacles, and plants and borders well-trimmed and weeded.

It would help if you kept the entrance area of your home free from clutter and barriers. Entrances often become storage areas for coats, shoes, boots and scarves and rather than hanging these on pegs or leaving them in a pile on the floor, build or create some storage areas, so they are shut away. If your door opens onto a wall, hang a picture of a view so that when someone enters the home, it gives the impression of space.

Welcome energy into your home by placing a bowl of crystals or a vase of flowers inside your front door. As well as looking visually attractive, they help to ease the flow of energy into the home as they blend the outside 'yin' of the natural world with the interior 'yang' of your home. Crystals and flowers can have specific meanings, so to attract wealth, use Carnelian or Citrine crystals, as these crystals are associated with money and good fortune. If you are placing flowers in your home, ensure they have plenty of water, and that dead leaves and flowers are removed immediately.

Energy Flow

Once the energy has entered your home, you want it to circulate and flow freely around your interior space. You don't want it to flow straight back out again. One way to keep the energy flowing inside your home is to minimize straight lines. Energy likes curves as curves allow it to move slowly in free-flowing shapes like in the natural world. When faced with a straight line, energy tends to move very quickly down the line. A common problem I see, especially in the UK, is a long straight hallway immediately inside the front door, which often leads to a back door. This kind of house design can cause problems as energy will flow into the home, down the hall, and straight back out again; bad news if you want to attract a flow of positive and beneficial energy throughout your house.

It is easy to cure this by creating curves in your hallway. This can be done by placing items of furniture, potted plants, side tables and ornaments at strategic places down your hall, creating a curved path. Again, you don't need to overdo it as you don't want the hall to look cluttered, but a large bamboo plant on one side and a small chair and side table further down the hallway on the other will work wonders in slowing the flow of energy as it enters your home. The same is true for any room in your house. Rather than having furniture pushed against walls and at right angles to each other piece, pull it away from the walls and angle it, so there are no sharp corners. If energy can flow, it will linger longer.

Clearing the Clutter

One of the easiest ways in which you can attract harmony, balance and good luck to your life is to have a home that is clean, well maintained and free of clutter. In doing this, you are automatically helping to refresh and revitalize your home's positive energy, helping it flow and circulate more easily. Think about how you feel after having a relaxing bath or spending a few days giving your body a detox. This is how your home feels once you have swept away the cobwebs, polished the floors, repainted the front door and mended the leaky tap driving you mad for the last few months. It feels better and refreshed, and the energy inside is more positive.

Walk around your home, noting anything that does not work as it should. Ensure that anything not in good repair is mended or replaced as soon as possible. This includes not only the fabric of the house but ornaments, clocks and pottery. If we live with broken items, then we signal to the Universe that we do not have the money to mend or replace them. We are making do

Move any boxes, papers, or anything you do not regularly use to somewhere safe and out of the way. If you have anything you don't need, give it away or sell it, which has the added advantage of automatically bringing money into your life. When moving items, do not store them in the corner of the room, in a little-used room or under the bed. Energy needs to circulate throughout your home, and if you block it, you may have difficulties in the area of your life where the blockage is.

Give everything a polish to make it shine, paying particular attention to any glass or crystals in your home as these surfaces can get cloudy. Cleaning and polishing your belongings recharges the energy in your home and adds sparkle to your life.

Once you have decluttered your house, walk around it with an incense or smudging stick, giving thanks for your home's security and happiness.

Focus on your hopes and desires for the coming few months and ask your home for its help and support as you work towards your dreams.

ENHANCEMENTS

Once you have balanced and harmonized the energy in your home, you can stimulate and promote positive energy in your environment to attract good fortune and abundance to your life. Sometimes, if you want to attract abundance in a particular area of your life, you may want to place a Feng Shui enhancement to give the energy an additional lift. This works the same way as having your hair done if you have a special occasion to go to or buying a new outfit. You already look good because you care for yourself but want to add some extra sparkle. Pretty much anything can be used as a wealth enhancement, providing that you place it intending to bring about good fortune, but in the main, they fall into these broad categories.

LIGHT ENHANCEMENTS

Light adds brightness to any neglected or dark area in the home, helping to attract positive energy into dark spaces. Light cures include crystal spheres which can be hung from red thread or ribbons from the ceiling, mirrors which can be placed on a wall to open up the room, candles placed on their own or in groups and lamps, either hanging from the ceiling or placed on tables or other furniture. When placing light enhancements in a space, the principle to follow is to ensure that the light enhancement does not overpower the space. If light enhancements are too large for the space, they can send energy pinging all over the place. Always ensure light enhancements are proportional to the space in which they are situated.

SOUND ENHANCEMENTS

Sound enhancements are very effective for clearing away negative energy, so they are good to use if you have been experiencing bad luck in your finances. Sound enhancements include wind chimes and bells. Wind Chimes should be hung where they can naturally catch the movement of energy and, for the maximum effect, should be hung from a red ribbon or thread.

Scent Enhancements

Scent enhancements are perfect for harmonizing energy as they have the advantage of being able to be controlled. You can decide how much or how little of a scent you want to promote in a space. Candles, incense, wax melts, oils, room mists and flowers all make great scent enhancements.

Moving Enhancements

Movement is a potent enhancement for stimulating energy. Moving enhancements include flowing water like a fountain or water feature, smoke from incense burners, whirligigs and mobiles.

Colour Enhancements

The use of colour is a very powerful and easy enhancement you can make to your home. Positive coloured objects that you can place in spaces in your home are coloured crystals, bowls, vases, boxes and pictures. The colours associated most closely with wealth and good fortune are red, purple and yellow.

Wealth Enhancements

Certain objects are renowned for bringing good fortune into the home. These include bamboo flutes, coins, animal ornaments such as toads, elephants, and crystals. Specific crystals for wealth and prosperity are Carnelian and Citrine.

EVALUATION

Always ask yourself if what you're doing today is getting you closer to where you want to be tomorrow. –Paulo Coelho

Life passes by quickly, and as one day is very often like another, it is easy to miss or not register some of the amazing gifts the Universe provides. This is because when we wait for a specific event or situation, we do not notice the small steps and actions that occur on the way. If we are going on a long journey, we focus on the destination, not the towns and villages we pass on the way, but each of those towns and villages is a sign that we are one mile closer to where we want to be. If we are dieting for our summer vacation, we may be aiming for a weight loss of twenty pounds, but that twenty pounds is made up of many small increments that we do not celebrate. When we have decided to become a money magnet, we expect all the Universe's riches and prosperity to be made available to us immediately. We can become frustrated if our life does not change straight away, but change, more often than not, is made up of a series of tiny changes, not a significant life-changing event.

I'm telling you this so that you do not become disheartened and give up when life does not change in the way that you want immediately. I always find it useful to note the changes that happen regularly. A good way of doing this is to write them down in a journal at the end of each day or the end of a week. Once a month, you can look back and be amazed at all the small gifts the Universe has provided that you would otherwise have missed.

The compliment a line manager or co-worker gave us for a job well done which bolstered our confidence and got us noticed at work. The space that became available in the high street as we drove to the shops, which meant that we did not have to pay a few pounds for parking in the car park. The coffee and cake that our friend bought us for listening to their problems saved us the money we would otherwise have spent. The offer in our email inbox which resulted in us reviewing our monthly utility payments and reducing them considerably. The newspaper article that we read which spurred us into action to embark on a side hustle that has started bringing in some additional money. The new hairstyle that our hairdresser suggested which has made us feel like a million dollars. The pound coin we found on the street. Yes, they are tiny and would have normally passed unnoticed, but each one is taking us one step closer to our dreams. And every step, however small, is worth celebrating.

But there is one more step that we need to practice, which is just as important as celebrating the successes. And that is to be grateful for them. And to show to the Universe that we are grateful by practising gratitude. In the same way that we would have thanked our friend for the coffee they bought or the co-worker for the compliment they paid, we need to say thank you to the Universe. The more we truly appreciate what we have, the more of the same we will receive.

An added benefit to practising gratitude is that if we appreciate something, it stops us worrying about something else. It is impossible to be appreciative and anxious at the same time. Every moment we spend in gratitude and appreciation is a moment we are not spending in anxiety and worry. We are drawing what we desire to ourselves, not what we fear. If we are thankful for whatever we receive, however small and seemingly insignificant it may feel, then before we know it, we are manifesting money constantly. We have created a money magnet mindset.

We now have all the tools at our disposal to create a money magnet mindset. There is no excuse. We can start right now on the journey to creating the life that we want and deserve. One that is filled with wealth, prosperity and abundance. Before we finish, let us remind ourselves of some of the key messages we need to keep in our minds.

1

What we desire is created twice, once in our mind and then in reality.

2

We have the same rights and opportunities for wealth and abundance as everyone else.

3

We must be clear about what we want.

4

We must strive to display positive behaviours always, for positivity attracts positivity.

5

We must take action now. There may never be a perfect time, but anytime is the right time.

6

We must not stop, however challenging life may be. Those who win are the ones who never give up.

7

Life is not a competition. There is no need to compare ourselves to others because we are living our best life.

8

When we ask the Universe for help, the Universe will always listen, although it may not provide the gift we expect

9

The more we appreciate what we have been given, the more we will have to be thankful for.

I hope that you have enjoyed this book. For more information on how you can create a money magnet mindset go to www.moneymagnetmindset.co.uk

If you are interested in learning more about Feng Shui, and how you can incorporate this into your life to attract what you desire, visit www.fengshuielements.co.uk where you will find lots of free information and resources.

www.ingramcontent.com/pod-product-compliance
Lightning Source LLC
Chambersburg PA
CBHW060220050426
42446CB00013B/3127